IMAGES
of America

STARVED ROCK STATE PARK

THE WORK OF THE CCC
ALONG THE I&M CANAL

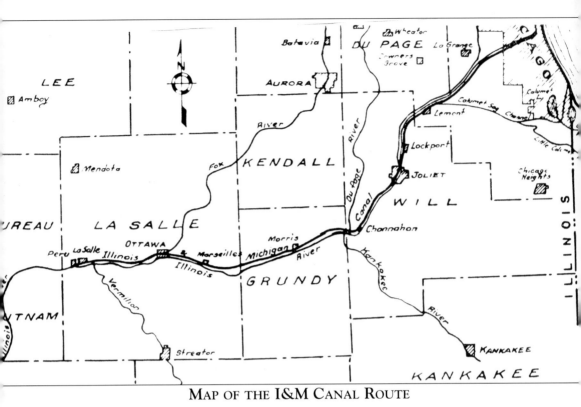

MAP OF THE I&M CANAL ROUTE

CAMP LOCATIONS

Starved Rock State Park Camps 614, 1609, and 2601, Utica
State Park 1-Camp 612, Willow Springs
State Park 2-Camp 631, Romeoville (located between Lemont and Lockport)
State Park 3-Camp 630, Morris
State Park 4-Camp 613, Marseilles
State Park 5-Camp 628 Buffalo Rock State Park (west of Ottawa)

CONTACT THE AUTHORS:
Gaylord Building Historic Site
200 West Eighth Street
Lockport, IL 60441
(815) 838-4830
(815) 588-1100
Fax (815) 588-1101

IMAGES
of America

STARVED ROCK
STATE PARK

THE WORK OF THE CCC
ALONG THE I&M CANAL

Dennis H. Cremin and
Charlene Giardina

ARCADIA

First Printed 2002.
Reprinted 2003.

Published by Arcadia Publishing,
an imprint of Tempus Publishing, Inc.
Charleston SC, Chicago, Portsmouth NH,
San Francisco

Printed in Great Britain.

Library of Congress Catalog Card Number: 2002105016

For all general information contact Arcadia Publishing at:
Telephone 843-853-2070
Fax 843-853-0044
E-Mail sales@arcadiapublishing.com

For customer service and orders:
Toll-Free 1-888-313-2665

Visit us on the internet at http://www.arcadiapublishing.com

Illinois Department of Natural Resources

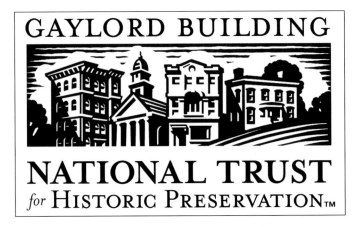

National Trust for Historic Preservation

CONTENTS

ACKNOWLEDGMENTS

The authors are indebted to many individuals and organizations for their assistance in the preparation of this book. The National Archives contributed CCC work reports and photographs. John M. Lamb, Director of the Lewis University Canal and Regional History Special Collection, and Special Collections Librarian Mary Ann Atkins shared their photo collection. Photographer John Voss provided contemporary photographs that document CCC structures along the canal route. CCC alumni Aaron Hill, Stephen Palco, and John Prazen supplied invaluable camp pictures. Local historian Mabel Hrpcha offered her photographic collection which broadened this investigation. We are beholden to Steve Potter for allowing us to feature his postcard collection of Starved Rock State Park.

John Daly, Director of the Illinois State Archives, sent us official state documents. Scholar Philip E. DeTurk offered information about camp newsletters. Julie Borden of Northwestern University, Theodore Karamanski of Loyola University in Chicago, Ann Keating of North Central College, Vince Michael of the School of the Art Institute of Chicago, Mary Tano of the Illinois and Michigan Canal National Heritage Corridor Commission, and Dr. James H. Cremin, provided timely assistance. Executive Director Rose Bucciferro of the Will County Historical Society lent her support and encouragement.

We value the oral history interviews with members of the CCC, including John Prazen and Melvin Keith Bost. Special thanks are due to Mickie Fisher and members of the National Association of CCC Alumni, Local Chapter 77, who shared insightful information. All the personal collections and memories inspired each of us who worked on the project.

The IDNR staff at Starved Rock State Park, especially Jon Blum and Toby Miller, generously shared their collection. David Carr, Hal Hassen, Joe Hennessy, Dan Bell and Jill Jackson lent their assistance throughout the process. National Trust for Historic Preservation staff Ann Hintze, Pat Chinderle, Bill Swanson, and Bette Nelson, assisted with the exhibit and public programs. University interns John Holevoet and Mary Sandgrin and volunteer Justine Lamb contributed their time and talents. Special recognition is owed to Judith Richardson for her assistance in proofreading and editing. The authors extend our deepest appreciation to everyone.

INTRODUCTION

The idea for a publication on the role of the Civilian Conservation Corps grew out of an exhibit, *Civilian Conservation Corps along the Illinois & Michigan Canal: A Work in Progress*, at the Gaylord Building in Lockport, IL. The project originated from the educational partnership at the Gaylord Building Historic Site between the National Trust for Historic Preservation and the Illinois Department of Natural Resources (IDNR). It ran from August 2001 to May 2002. One of the exhibit's goals was to gather additional research material. As new material came to light, we modified the exhibit. The Illinois Humanities Council partially funded the effort, and their Road Scholar Program supported Kay Rippelmeyer-Tippy's public presentation at the Gaylord Building.

A map of the Illinois and Michigan Canal Parkways System 1938, provided the point of departure for research on the topic. The map depicted an astonishing complex of recreational sites connected by a highway along the canal's old towpath. In 1933 the I & M Canal had officially closed, and waterborne commerce had moved to the Illinois Waterway. This provided an opportunity to transform the commercial waterway into a recreational resource. The authors' goal has been to increase awareness of the role of the CCC along this scenic American landscape.

Although monumental in scale, it is easy to overlook the CCC's contribution to transforming the landscape of this part of Illinois. For example, the men drained sections of the canal and cleaned it out, moved mature trees for conspicuous display, and built roads that connected municipal, county, and state park sites. This book commemorates these CCC efforts along the canal, which include work on some of the colossal remnants of the old canal.

At the core of the CCC story was the Great Depression. Particularly hard hit by the nationwide economic reversal were thousands of young men who could not find employment. The Civilian Conservation Corps recruited single men ranging in age from 17 to 28. The young men dressed in uniforms and lived in barracks. The program ran from 1933 to 1942. Coupled with the human misery, there was the condition of the American landscape, which had been ravaged by deforestation, soil erosion, and industrial pollution. Addressing these problems as a part of the New Deal, Franklin D. Roosevelt initiated the Emergency Conservation Work Act, the public works program popularly known as the Civilian Conservation Corps.

Roosevelt's concern for conservation and restoration of the American landscape reflected the efforts of his distant cousin, President Theodore Roosevelt, who earlier reserved millions of acres of land, which were closed to commercial development. The story of the CCC underscores the connection between the canal landscape and political and labor history. It became the most popular of the New Deal programs. In 1935 it counted 500,000 men in its ranks.

Much of this study centers on Starved Rock State Park, which has been the most notable reminder of the work of the CCC. The three companies at Starved Rock, companies 614, 2601, and 1609, transformed the park and expanded its usage. The five camps situated along the old I & M Canal included State Park 1-Camp 612, State Park 2-Camp 631, State Park 3-Camp 630, State Park 4-Camp 613, and State Park 5-Camp 628. The men in these camps built the I & M Canal Parkway, while also accomplishing numerous other conservation projects. Like the companies at Starved Rock State Park, these five played the greatest role in changing the appearance and use of the areas along the route of the canal in the 1930s.

Since the late 1960s, many people have been aware of the grass roots efforts to create the I & M Canal State Trail (1974) and subsequently the Illinois and Michigan Canal National Heritage Corridor (1984). However, the story of the CCC's early accomplishments and contributions to the Canal Parkway System had gotten lost—with the exception of the impressive lodge at Starved Rock State Park.

The photographic record for these camps and the brief review of the history of the canal feature a number of historical and contemporary images of Lockport, Illinois. This focus reflects the research agenda of the Gaylord Building Historic Site and its attempt to make the building's environs intelligible to visitors. The educational staff encourages readers to visit Lockport and the other sites along the Illinois and Michigan Canal.

One
STARVED ROCK
STATE PARK
HISTORICAL OVERVIEW

Beautifully situated along the south bank of the Illinois River is Starved Rock State Park. Less than 100 miles from Chicago, it attracts hundreds of thousands of visitors who walk along its trails, dine in its fine restaurant, and glory in its panoramic views. A hike up the sandstone butte or an exploration of any of the 18 canyons promises an exhilarating experience.

The Illinois River and its tributaries attracted the first people to this area. As early as 8000 BC Native American cultures thrived here. From 1500 to 1700, a number of Illiniwek, a confederation of many sub-tribes, lived here. One of these sub-tribes, the Kaskaskias, established a village with a population of as many as 7,000 along the bank of the Illinois River across from the current park. In 1673 French explorers Louis Jolliet and Father Jacques Marquette canoed up the river below the great rock. Marquette returned in 1675 to found the Mission of the Immaculate Conception, the region's first Christian mission, at the Indian village. In the winter of 1682–1683, the French built Fort St. Louis atop Starved Rock.

Starved Rock State Park derives its name from a Native American legend of injustice and retribution. In the 1760s, toward the end of the French and Indian War, Chief Pontiac of the Ottawa tribe was slain by an Illiniwek while attending a tribal council. According to the legend, during one of the battles to avenge his killing, a band of Illiniwek, under attack by a band of Potawatomi (allies of the Ottawa), sought refuge atop a 125-foot sandstone butte. The Ottawa and Potawatomi surrounded the butte and held their ground until the Illiniwek died of starvation, giving rise to the name "Starved Rock."

In the 1890s, private ventures at Starved Rock tapped some of the recreational potential of the site. Starved Rock was developed for vacationers, complete with a hotel, dance pavilion, and swimming area. In 1911 the State of Illinois purchased the site, making it the state's first recreational park. In the 1930s, the Civilian Conservation Corps placed three camps at Starved Rock State Park and began what has become a remarkable legacy of their labors.

All of the images are postcards and are provided courtesy of Steve Potter.

In the 1890s entrepreneurs capitalized on the charm of the natural features along the Illinois River by building Starved Rock Hotel. The hotel was later torn down. In the 1930s, the CCC built the present lodge on the bluff overlooking the river. (c. 1905)

This was the entrance to Starved Rock. The site had long been favored for vacations because of its extraordinary beauty and the allure of its French and Native American heritage. (*c.* 1915)

THE CAMPGROUND AT STARVED ROCK, LASALLE COUNTY, ILL.

Park boats like these made short excursions on the Illinois River. (*c.* 1909)

The paddle-wheeler, *Lola*, is depicted at the base of Starved Rock. The natural features of Starved Rock dominate this section of the Illinois River. (*c.* 1910)

Within the eastern section of the park is Horse Shoe Canyon, long a popular destination. It is one of many with waterfalls cascading down to the rocky canyon floors. The canyons are cool, shady, and overgrown with ferns, vines, and flowering plants. (c. 1910)

Formal trails and rustic bridges assisted these men in exploring the park's many points of interest. Explorers hiked to places with fanciful names such as Skeleton Cave or the Cave of the Winds. (c. 1925)

Path to Wild Cat Canyon, midway between Horseshoe Canyon and Starved Rock near Ottawa, Utica, La Salle and Peru, Ill.

This lookout from Wild Cat Canyon featured a view of the Illinois River.

In the western section of the park, the bluffs receded from the river. On the broad terrace were the main parking area, refreshment concessions, and swimming area. (*c.* 1930)

Deer Park, adjacent to Starved Rock, featured heavily wooded grounds with a deep gorge carved into the St. Peter's sandstone by a tributary of the Vermilion River. Tradition has it that the Native Americans used the park's canyons as enclosures for deer, which furnished the winter's meat supply. Today the area is Matthiessen State Park. (*c.* 1910)

Buffalo Rock State Park was another regional destination on the north bank of the Illinois River. It takes its name from a huge, tree-topped rock, rising 100 feet above the river. This charming park features a picnic shelter, winding trails, and majestic views. The park was the location for CCC camp 628. (*c.* 1940)

Greetings from BEAUTIFUL STARVED ROCK STATE PARK ILLINOIS

© CURT TEICH & CO., INC.

This promotional postcard highlights both the scenic beauty of the park and its CCC constructed lodge. (c. 1945)

Since it was built, the rustic beauty of Starved Rock Lodge has been a major attraction within the park. Its elevation provides breathtaking views of the Illinois River and access to Starved Rock. (c. 1950)

The popularity of Starved Rock State Park and the lodge gave rise to the adjacent hotel, which offered an alternative to sleeping in the small cabins. (c. 1945)

This interior view of Starved Rock Lodge depicts the massive fireplace and rustic furnishings. The CCC built the fireplace and it remains the central feature of the lodge. (c. 1955)

Two

STARVED ROCK
STATE PARK
CAMP 614

The story of company 614 at Starved Rock State Park is in part the story of a federal program. The CCC grew out of Franklin D. Roosevelt's interests in employing young men and conserving the nation's resources. During its nine years of existence, around 2.5 million young men passed though its camps. The program was extremely popular with both those who had enrolled in the Emergency Conservation Work and the general public.

Robert Fechner, the first director of the CCC, wrote, "The major objectives of this new venture in social relief were to give jobs to hundreds of thousands of discouraged and undernourished young men, idle through no fault of their own, to build up these young men physically and spiritually, and to start the nation on a sound conservation program which would conserve and expand our timber resources, increase recreational opportunities and reduce the annual toll taken by forest fire, disease, pests, soil erosion and floods." The United States Army was soon engaged in setting up camps for hundreds of thousands of young men.

The annals of the CCC at Starved Rock State Park reveal that company 614 had the briefest tenure. Yet their experience reflected that of many camps across the nation. The company was made up of around 200 men. The United States Army set up and administered the camps. The Army was the only agency capable of enlisting and moving the thousands of enrollees from induction centers to work camps. The advisors for the camps in this area were provided by the Department of the Interior. Company 614 originated at Jefferson Barracks, Missouri, later moving to Starved Rock State Park. The camp eventually relocated to the Illini National Forest at Murphysboro, Jackson County, IL. Most of the images in this chapter were preserved in a scrapbook kept by Captain Taylor, who eventually became company commander.

Images are courtesy of Starved Rock State Park unless otherwise noted.

Company 614 was photographed shortly after their arrival at Utica, Illinois.

orps
No. 614

Capt. E. F. Carey
Commanding

When they first arrived, the enrollees of Camp 614 were housed in large tents. Eventually, wooden barracks would be constructed.

The men of the barracks are seen here in their uniforms. Notable is the fact that a few African Americans were enrollees of this camp. With some exceptions, nation-wide segregation of CCC camps was the rule.

The United States Army operated the camps with order and discipline.

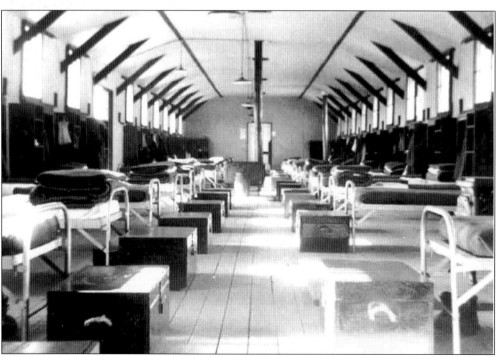

Aaron Hill is pictured here at 18 years of age. (Courtesy of Aaron Hill.)

Captain Taylor eventually commanded company 614 and was often seen with his black German Shepherd. Many camps had pets or company mascots.

Captain Taylor, pictured on the left, is seen with an unidentified officer.

The staff from the dispensary, known as "Witch Doctors' Lodge," is seen here. Every enrollee had a physical examination and inoculations. The staff provided first aid and treated other minor maladies as they arose. For many enrollees, the CCC provided their first encounter with professional health care.

The enrollees were in the camp year round. These men are standing in the rain. In spite of the sometimes challenging conditions, the corps was popular with the men. By the end of 1935, enrollees nationwide numbered 505,782, and there were over 2,650 camps in operation across the nation.

During their work at Starved Rock State Park, the enrollees completed projects from the bluffs down to the river's edge.

The trucks were used to transport men to work and leisure activities in the surrounding area. Driving a truck was considered one of the better jobs in camp.

The CCC constructed miles of trails and built many benches along the way.

The men built many recreational shelters within the park.

When not working, the men enjoyed leisure time in the recreation hall.

The men often gathered in their barracks to relax.

Most camps fielded a baseball team, which would play other camps, semi-professional teams, and local municipal teams.

Each of the camps had a canteen that sold candy and soft drinks. Since prohibition had been repealed, men of age could buy 3.2 percent beer.

Some enrollees knew how to play instruments and created small ensembles. The groups would often be called on to perform at special functions such as the camp's anniversary. Some camps provided musical instruction to enrollees. They were taught by teachers employed by the Works Progress Administration.

Three

STARVED ROCK
STATE PARK
CAMP 2601

Camp 2601 originated at Fort Sheridan in Chicago on July 16 ,1934, and in August moved to Starved Rock. They took the place of Camp 614. As in other companies, the enrollees who enrolled in the first couple of years of the program were unmarried, unemployed male citizens between the ages of 18 and 25. The age range was later expanded to include men from age 17 to 28. Many malnourished and illiterate men enrolled for a six-month-long enlistment. Eventually the men could extend their terms of enlistment. The junior enrollees earned $30 a month, with a substantial portion, between $22 and $25, sent home to dependent families. Men could advance within the ranks of the corps and receive additional pay.

In addition to their stipend for the five-day work week, the young men received three full meals a day, lodging, clothes, footwear, inoculations, other medical and dental care, and, at their option, vocational, academic, or recreational instruction. Many took advantage of the 8th Grade equivalency course work. The majority were inexperienced or wholly ignorant of the fundamentals of the tasks ahead, especially those related to the reclamation of the natural and cultural heritage.

In Illinois there were some 50 CCC camps, with two dozen or more operating in the peak year of 1935. For the large camps, the optimum work force varied from 180 to 200 enrollees. Some larger Illinois state parks had long-term or multiple projects, including White Pines State Park in Ogle County and Pere Marquette State Park in Jersey County. Starved Rock State Park in La Salle County was one of these larger camps.

All images are courtesy of Stephen Palco.

Pictured here is the entrance sign to Camp La Salle Company 2601.

The camp newsletter, *Canyon Echo*, March 30, 1936, reported that "2601 Company on August 9th, 1934, at 8:15 in the morning, the company left Fort Sheridan and started the journey to Starved Rock. Arriving in the town of Utica, about 4:25 in the evening, the men made a hurried trip to our present location. This was a day to be long remembered by the men of our company. Being assigned to our barracks was the first step to be taken. The company received its name the following day, 'Camp La Salle.'"

When camps were forming, men stayed in tents until wooden buildings were constructed.

Large CCC camps had at least 11 buildings, including four barracks, officers' quarters, garages, a mess hall, recreation hall, infirmary, latrine, and shower building.

The mess hall was central to the lives of the men in camp. Most men gained weight and ate well in the camp.

Although not fancy, the buildings in the camps served the needs of the enrollees.

This photograph shows Barracks #7.

Most of the enrollees were accustomed to the proverbial Saturday night bath. However, given the heavy outdoor labor, frequent bathing was required.

Captain E. Pytlak commanded the camp from April 25, 1935, to September 30, 1936.

Officers at Camp La Salle from 1935 to 1936 are seen here, with Captain Pytlak pictured at the far right.

Seen here are National Park Service forestry advisors. From the newsletter, *Canyon Echo*, Camp La Salle, Utica Co. 2601, January 21, 1936: "If there is anything that makes a camp go round and round and come out here (on top) it is the cooperation of the NPS and the Army. The willingness to cooperate is one of the rarest and finest attributes to be found in any organization. Fortunately for all of us, Supt. Ehringer and Capt. Pytlak are blessed with this faculty, and consequently Co. 2601 is operated with an absence of friction that is a joy to everybody connected with CCC work at this park."

"The Gang" from Company 2601, as Stephen Palco referred to them, is seen here. In the above picture, Palco stands in the back row, second from the left.

Seen here are Stephen Palco's buddies, "Berry & Hammer," at the flagpole.

The camp's pet groundhog is captured in this photograph.

44

"Kid Cherry" poses for a photograph.

"Kid Suey" smiles for the camera.

Given the six-month terms of enlistment, the camps were continuously training new enrollees. This often created tension in the camps. Established friends parted and newcomers often were daunted by their new surroundings and circumstances. These were the new enrollees to camp 2601.

The men built a garage for company 2601.

This work detail called themselves the "Stone Cutting Gang."

Stephen Palco called this "Sipe's Hell Hole." The CCC enrollees did most of their work by hand, using simple tools, picks and wheelbarrows.

"Bing" posed for a shot in a picnic area. As noted in the *Canyon Echo*, March 30, 1938, on the topic of the coming new enrollment: "Most of you are no doubt glad you are going home. But do not forget what your enrollment in the CCC has done for you. It has developed your body, set you out with the idea you are a full grown man. Helped you to help yourself. To look into the future with a new and brighter aspect."

A work detail gathered at a site; Stephen Palco is seen in the first row, second from right. Scottie Buchanan, Jr. wrote the following lyrics in *Canyon Echoes*, March 30, 1936: "We will work, we will strive to help beautify this place of ours. We will try, we will conquer, Sing our way to the top."

Even in cold weather the work whistle would ring out. Sometimes conditions were such that it was impossible to work. At those times that the camp would be improved, shoes polished, and the interiors of the camp's buildings cleaned.

Stephen Palco and other enrollees worked on the bridge in Wildcat Canyon.

The *Canyon Echo*, March 30, 1936, reported: "The bridges to be found spanning all the outlets and flowing streams of the canyons are real pieces of work. There we can sit and rest on the span of the bridges and get a real view of the beautiful canyons. The Wildcat Canyon Bridge now under construction will be one of the best in the park when it will be completed."

The enrollees made these shelters out of limestone and large timbers. The structure featured two large fireplaces.

The Camp Log, December 15, 1935: "The National Park Service office, under the guidance of Supt. Ehringer, designs all our structures. Ours is the only camp that enjoys this special privilege. The excellent type of work accomplished is due largely to the fact that the construction department, under Senior Supt. Latimer, can cooperate at close hand with the department of design."

"Kid Boris" is dressed here in his civilian clothes while at the camp.

2601 Camp enrollees enjoyed a trip away from the camp and its projects. Some of the campers went to Brookfield Zoo or the Century of Progress fair in Chicago, 1933 and 1934.

An enrollee is photographed at the wheel of a topless car.

The enrollees enjoyed playing pool in the recreation hall. Men could also take advantage of books in the library, educational courses, and crafts such as leather working or carving.

Pictured are eight members of 2601's baseball team. From *The Canyon Flash*, September 12, 1935: "Company 2601 played one of their opponents in the league, Co. 1609. The game ended with a score of 2 to 1 in favor of Company 1609. Although Bartnik pitched a one-hit game, two runs were scored by the opposition due to errors. Shang of Co 1609 allowed 9 hits and only one run."

Four

STARVED ROCK
STATE PARK
CAMP 1609

Civilian Conservation Company 1609 had the greatest impact on Starved Rock State Park. Originating on June 9, 1933, at Fort Sheridan, Illinois, it moved for a short time to Camp Readstown, Wisconsin, and relocated to Starved Rock State Park on December 15, 1933. They built their camp on the elevated southeastern section of the park. Companies 614 and 2601 were located close to the Illinois River, rather than on the bluff.

During its six years in the park, 1609 worked to reduce fire hazards and conserve natural resources. Significantly for the park, major attention would be paid to creating recreational amenities, including over 25 miles of trails, Starved Rock Lodge, and a parking area for several hundred cars. The enrollees would eventually landscape all of the structures and set out more than 1.5 million plants throughout the park. They established a nursery that produced thousands of trees, including oak and walnut, and restored many neglected varieties.

This camp was the longest lived of the camps at Starved Rock State Park. It won awards and saw much of the work in the park to completion. Albert N. Corpening, Chaplain Third Sub-District, reflected in *The Camp Log* March 13, 1936: "Right now I am thinking about Camp Starved Rock, its location, its officers, and its men. First, it is one of the most beautiful camps of the seventeen that I have served. In summer, lawns, flowers, and well-kept buildings with the Stars and Stripes flying from the finest flag-pole that has come under my observation display their beauty for passers-by and home folks." By all accounts it was a special camp.

Images are courtesy of Starved Rock State Park and John Prazen.

The Camp Log for December 15, 1934, reported: "One year ago this camp was a rather barren place with very few conveniences. In a year's time it has been built up to such an extent that Co. 1609 rates very high among the top notchers in the entire Sixth Corps Area. While a number of you fellows do not realize the vast improvements that have been made, due to your entering Camp within the last few months, a short talk with any of the few remaining "Charter members" will prove interesting. Captain Smith is constantly promoting an improvement program for the betterment of Co. 1609. Remember this is your Camp—and it should be a matter of personal pride to keep everything in A-1 shape."

John Prazen of Camp 1609 commented in an oral interview on the role of the United States Army on camp life. He recalled, "We didn't march around in step or anything like that. We didn't have guns, but the discipline was there." He continued, "You had to keep your barracks, you know. I went into the Navy later on. I don't think the Navy was as clean as we were at that camp. I mean, you had to be clean. Like, I say, when we left for work our bunks had to be lined up with a string."

Men from the Department of the Interior oversaw the work projects in the camp. Some of these men, like George Walkey, pictured at right and on the left in the picture below, were younger and entered into an easy camaraderie with the enrollees. (Courtesy of John Prazen.)

John Prazen is pictured with a mallet and chisel. With him are Eli Maurice and Slusarek. Prazen wished that he had kept a diary. "There was so much going on, and we were all the same age. There were a few veterans of WWI, and they were the barracks' leaders. They would try to get us to go to bed at 10 o'clock curfew. Occasionally, there would be a poker game or something, and a veteran would tell us to cut it out. And then he'd get mad and say, 'I'm gonna get the chief foreman after you; you're not taking my orders.' And we would all get tired of that." (Courtesy of John Prazen.)

John Prazen recalled that there was a barber shop in the camp. "We'd stop in the doorway and we'd say, "Hey Maurice, better go to barber school. Look at the steps you put in that guy's hair." Eli Maurice was the barber pictured here.

One of George Walkey's work details is seen here. Pictured from the right are Eli Maurice, John Prazen, and John Rivett. The other two men are not identified. From the December 15, 1935, *Camp Log*: "We have built over 25 miles of trails that are the equal of any in the country. There are trails adapted to every class, from the most casual stroller to the most energetic hiking enthusiast." (Courtesy of John Prazen.)

From the December 15, 1935, *Camp Log*: "A 25-foot towboat and a large barge were built to transport all the material necessary for construction along the river trail. In over two years of operation our navy has never caused or met with an accident." (Courtesy of John Prazen.)

According to Prazen, this was one of the first boats to go through the lock on the Illinois Waterway. (Courtesy of John Prazen.)

The Camp Log, January 15, 1935, quotes Harry Weis of Milwaukee, "From December, 1933, until July 1934, our company was at Starved Rock State Park, Utica, IL. I have made lifelong friends in the CCC. Aside from the building of many worthwhile projects the CCC is bringing our nation closer. Today as I walk down the streets and meet many CCC's who were bunking with me I hear the same statement, 'Wish I was back in Camp.' I have yet to hear from, or talk to, the discharged CCC from Co. 1609 who does not wish he was back in camp—wish that some means of re-enlistment be made." Eventually it did become possible for the men to reenlist.

This is the nearly completed river trail. (Courtesy of John Prazen.)

George Walkey's crew is pictured here on the CCC built-barge. *The Camp Log*, February 16, 1935, reported a quote from M.M. Latimore, Senior Project Superintendent: "The point was brought out that most CCC men are getting valuable experience along many lines while on the job."

From *The Camp Log*, December 15, 1935: "We have developed this park so that the tens of thousands of people who visit it each year can easily enjoy its manifold beauties. The first step in making the park accessible was the construction of walkable trails."

The Camp Log, December 20, 1935, reported that Lt. Governor Donovan spoke at Camp Starved Rock. "He stressed the fact that the good training received in CCC camp would be brought out in the future when enrollees applied for and received employment. The expenditure for CCC Camps was compared with that of the large expenditures of another nature, and he said that the work being done here would be used by future generations and remain as the property of the State for the benefit of the people."

Here they are digging the foundations for Starved Rock Lodge. *The Canyon Echo*, February 26, 1937, noted that "The first step in this job was the erecting of forms and pouring the foundations. Next came the problem of fitting the logs so there would be no air spaces. This was solved by making the logs flat on top and bottom. Oakum was then tacked onto the flattened surfaces and each log spiked down with 13-inch spikes."

The camps were able to buy timber from surrounding farms. The men would go out, chop down the trees, and bring them to the camps. This provided the benefit of generating revenue for farmers, conserving the park's natural resources, and providing work for the men.

The Camp Log, December 15, 1935, reported: "In the area surrounding Starved Rock we have constructed a great log lodge and several log cabins. A parking area large enough for several thousand cars has been surfaced and fenced. A very unique parking area has been developed to

handle the cars of picnickers and campers in the newly developed campground. Sanitary facilities have been improved by the construction of a new toilet building equipped with showers and all modern conveniences."

This is the Lumber Yard, where enrollees used saws to cut logs for the lodge.

The men stacked logs in the lumber yard.

The men used some machines in the wood shop.

Details of men volunteered to quarry limestone at an unspecified site for use within Starved Rock State Park.

The Canyon Echo, March 30, 1936, reported: "The lodge up on the hill in the parking grounds is no doubt the park's pride. It has two of the most beautiful fireplaces in the entire country. Altho this project is still unfinished, it will be a masterpiece in lodge work when it is completed."

The Canyon Flash, September 12, 1935, reported: "The Log Lodge on the Camp grounds is nearing completion. The masonry work, under the direction of Wm. Zaker, will be finished within the next few days. The work done by the CCC on this project is marveled at and commented upon by all. The fireplace is acclaimed as the finest in the U.S."

The Camp Log, February 16, 1935, quoted M.M. Latimore, Senior Project Superintendent: "Work on the lodge in the campgrounds is progressing rapidly. An interesting item connected with this project is the building of a large stone fire-place, know to the men of this company as 'Boone' Adam's fire-place. 250 tons of Joliet limestone have been hauled from near Lemont to Starved Rock Park for the purpose of making this fire-place. The rock was quarried by Illinois Emergency Relief laborers and hauled to the Park by CCC men. This project is probably one of the most exacting in the Park and when completed will be a very impressive piece of masonry."

The CCC companies created significant changes to Starved Rock State Park. The location overlooking the Illinois River, which became part of the Illinois Waterway in 1933, presented spectacular vistas.

John Prazen from Camp 1609 reflected, "I used to go in the evening. There was a path and there was a rock that stood like Starved Rock, and you could see way down the river and across. And I'd go by myself; this was really peaceful. It was so quiet. . . . And many a time, I'd just go down there and sit, and I don't know, it was just nice being alone and sitting there."

Five
I & M CANAL
HISTORICAL OVERVIEW

One of the most enduring catalysts for change in the early 19th century in Northeastern Illinois was the Illinois and Michigan Canal. This 96.4 mile-long canal connected the Illinois River with Lake Michigan. The I & M Canal completed a chain of waterways from New York to New Orleans, including the Atlantic Ocean, Hudson River, Erie Canal, Great Lakes, Chicago River, I & M Canal, Illinois River, Mississippi River, and Gulf of Mexico.

The waterway transformed the native American landscape. It ushered in new ways of business, industry, and community. Since the first shovelful of Chicago dirt was turned by the hands of dignitaries on July 4th, 1836, the canal has been a constant reminder of this history.

During the era of westward expansion, early pioneer farmers and entrepreneurs made their way to the port of Chicago by wagon and by boat. Many looked forward to the day when the last link in a chain of waterways would hasten the journey between the Atlantic Ocean and the Gulf of Mexico. The call for a canal had been echoing across the prairies for centuries. In 1673 French Canadian explorers Louis Jolliet and Father Jacques Marquette declared that the tortuous portage through the leech-infested swamp at Chicago could be overcome by 1.5-mile canal.

The mere promise of a canal spurred the first permanent changes in the region. With hope, passion, and enormous energy, the first settlers cut down groves of trees and shaped them into fences, homes, and towns. Irish, German, and Scandinavian laborers dug the canal with picks and shovels. They also built impressive structures in Lockport, including the I & M Canal Commissioners Office, the Canal Warehouse (today the Gaylord Building Historic Site), and canal locks.

After overcoming shortages of men, money, and machines, the canal (60 feet wide, 6 feet deep) opened in 1848. Mule-drawn boats carried thousands of passengers and tons of cargo. Towns grew and prospered, though none more significantly than Chicago. The city emerged, and remains today unrivaled as the transportation crossroads and center of commerce in the Midwest.

Even with competition from the railroads, the canal paid for itself and helped develop the nation. In 1933 the I & M Canal closed and the Illinois Waterway opened. Today the route of the old canal links the natural, cultural, and industrial resources of the corridor.

Unless otherwise indicated, photographs are courtesy of the Lewis University Canal and Regional History Special Collection.

The story of the Gaylord Building in Lockport mirrors the history of the I & M Canal. Built in 1838, the original structure served as a construction depot for materials to dig the canal. When the canal opened in 1848, the building converted to a privately owned granary. In 1859 a three-story addition accommodated a general store. By the late 1880s, the building housed the Barrows Lock Manufacturing Company, reflecting an increase in industry along the canal. Descendants of George Gaylord, the owner from 1878–1883, restored the building. It re-opened in 1987, with a restaurant and exhibit galleries. Owned by the National Trust for Historic Preservation, the building houses exhibits and programs in partnership with the Illinois Department of Natural Resources. (c. 1880s)

The I & M Canal Headquarters in Lockport housed the offices of canal engineers and commissioners. On April 16, 1848, the building and grounds held hundreds of dignitaries and folks from towns up and down the canal. Everyone feasted and danced in celebration of the first boats to ply the waterway between Chicago and La Salle-Peru. Since 1969–1970, the building has been the home of the Will County Historical Society and I & M Canal Museum. (*c.* 1880s)

This sketch interprets the hustle and bustle of the Public Landing in Lockport. The landing is bordered by the Gaylord Building on the north and the Norton Building two blocks to the south. (Courtesy of the Canal Corridor Association. Sketch by Tom Willcockson, 1998.)

In 1859 businessman Hiram Norton replaced a modest wood structure with a massive 100 foot square limestone building. Built of the same locally quarried dolomite as the Gaylord Building, the site was a granary and store. This elevator stored the grain processed at his hydraulic mills across the canal. Today the Illinois State Museum Lockport Gallery occupies part of the Norton Building. (c. 1869)

The canal conveyed passenger and cargo boats, but it also helped supply water power to run mills. Hiram Norton's hydraulic mills ground flour, planed lumber and produced commercial paper. The complex was one of the largest in the country. The *Elizabeth* was one of Norton's boats. A CCC shelter marks the general location of the mill site in Lockport. (c. 1896)

The *Margaret* maneuvered a boat load of timber through Lock #6 at Channahon. Local trees fueled the lime kilns that produced hydraulic cement for canal foundations. Most of the building-quality timber came from Michigan and Wisconsin and piled up at boat slips in Chicago, waiting for delivery to the lumber mills. (*c.* 1900)

The *Nashota*, pictured at a Seneca grain elevator, is an example of the steamboats that used the canal after it was enlarged in 1871. A few mule drawn boats trod the towpath during this time as well. Visitors to Seneca can tour the M. J. Hogan Grain Elevator, a state park site, nearby. (c. 1900)

Parallel to the I & M Canal is the Rock Island Railroad and the four piers of the Vermillion Aqueduct. The bridge in the distance served the Illinois Central Railroad. (*c.* 1868)

A string of lake boats left the port of Chicago, ultimately destined for New York. This lithograph is from a Frank Lesley newspaper of 1874.

Even in the early days of the canal, Chicagoans enjoyed a leisurely excursion to Lockport's canal headquarters and back. These pleasure trips foreshadowed the days when the canal would be used exclusively for recreation. (c. 1910)

On this occasion men pulled the boat out of the lock at Channahon. During the early days of the canal, mules and horses towed the cargo and passenger boats. (c. 1900)

84

Morton Salt owned the steam-powered boat, *Niagara*, positioned between locks 3 and 4 in Joliet. In 1914 this boat made history by taking the last commercial cargo from the west end of the canal at La Salle to the headquarters in Lockport. (*c.* 1911)

The Sanitary and Ship Canal replaced the I & M Canal to Lockport with a channel over 20 feet deep. This canal is part of the Illinois Waterway, which replaced the I & M Canal in 1933. (c. 1895) (From left to right are the Des Plaines River, Sanitary & Ship Canal/Lockport Power House/Lock, Lockport Lock and Dam (1933), Deep Run Creek, and the original location of the Des Plaines River. The city of Lockport and the I & M Canal are out of view to the right.)

Six

CCC

AND THE

I&M CANAL PARKWAY

In 1933, the Illinois and Michigan Canal was officially replaced by the Illinois Waterway. This created an opportunity to transform the route of the old canal from an industrial, transportation corridor into a recreational resource. The beauty of the canal and the presence of the old tow path made it ideal for leisure use. This work was begun with the inauguration of Emergency Conservation Work in 1933.

During the succeeding five years, five camps developed bridle paths, foot trails, trailside shelters, comfort facilities, and boat docks, in addition to planting trees and shrubbery and constructing picnicking accommodations. The completion of the parkway pointed the way to the close consolidation of a compact system of five adjoining park areas: Fox River picnic areas; Gebhard Woods parks; Illini State Park; Buffalo Rock State Park; and Starved Rock State Park. Will County's McKinley Woods and several of the Cook County forest preserves. The whole region offered wonderful recreational opportunities.

Five camps, stretching from Willow Springs to La Salle, were constructed to house the young men committed to the monumental projects involving the Illinois and Michigan Canal route and the surrounding area. The five CCC camps were State Park 1 Camp 612, State Park 2 Camp 631, State Park 3 Camp 630, State Park 4 Camp 613, and State Park 5 Camp 628. Each company was composed of around 200 enrollees. As at the camps at Starved Rock State Park, these camps were under the direction of the United States Army and the work projects were directed by the Department of Interior. The images that follow provide an overview of the work of these companies.

Photographs are courtesy of the National Archives and Lewis University Canal and Regional History Special Collection.

The Civilian Conservation Corps built this parking lot and guard rails on Lockport's Public Landing. This view to the north shows the Gaylord Building Historic Site. (c. 1934) (Courtesy of the National Archives.)

The "CCC boys" built a stone wall for a parking area on Lockport's Public Landing. This view looking north shows Lockport's Ninth Street Bridge on the left and the close proximity of rail cars on the right. (Courtesy of the National Archives.)

This view of the old canal adjacent to Ninth Street in Lockport looking east shows the CCC delivering and spreading soil. (Courtesy of the National Archives.)

This image shows a footbridge being built across the I&M Canal. The bridge leads to the Lockport Shelter on Canal Street. Note the skaters in the foreground on the canal. (Courtesy of the National Archives.)

The enrollees worked at Lockport to clear the channel and control erosion. The young men planted material along the banks. The five camps along the canal did work similar to this up and down the canal's route. (Courtesy of the National Archives.)

The young men of the CCC drained and cleared out the debris in the canal. A young man in a canoe tries out the improved canal. (Courtesy of the National Archives.)

The industrial structures of Lockport's hydraulic basin shows "hilling up with scraper in preparing for planting to screen building." (Courtesy of the National Archives.)

This view looking northwest shows the industrial structures of Lockport's hydraulic basin. Later, the CCC would build the Lockport shelter on this site. (Courtesy of the National Archives.)

Enrollees constructed Lockport's shelter of limestone and wood at the hydraulic basin. It featured a fireplace and a covered seating area. (Courtesy of the National Archives.)

This view looking north from the canal footbridge near Twelfth Street in Lockport shows the canal during the process of clearing. It also showes the approximate water level to be maintained once the project was complete. (Courtesy of the National Archives.)

The enrollees created "Legion Park," north of Lockport, IL at the site of an old stone quarry. Today the park is owned by the Forest Preserve District of Will County and is named after the first permanent settler in the area, Armstead Runyon. The project supervisor wrote of this image, "shows tool house made from dilapidated shed. Bank to the right will be sloped. Dam to the left will be removed, thus giving a longer expanse of water." (Courtesy of the National Archives.)

The CCC restored Runyon Cemetery, in Lockport, Illinois. The Runyon family were the early settlers in this area. (Courtesy of the National Archives.)

The young men built many bridges. This one was constructed for vehicles at "Legion Park." (Courtesy of the National Archives.)

The National Park Service planned this fireplace shelter for Legion Park. This shelter has been torn down. (Courtesy of the National Archives.)

CCC workers uncover the remains of an old boat on the I & M Canal. In 1996, a flood drained the canal in Morris, revealing seven canal era boats. An archeological study and publication have helped to create an awareness and appreciation of this part of the canal's history. (Courtesy of the National Archives.)

Workers often constructed sheds along the canal to store tools instead of taking them back to the camp each night. This one was situated at the Channahon work site. (Lewis University Canal and Regional History Special Collection.)

This dragline outfit was used at Channahon. (Lewis University Canal and Regional History Special Collection.)

A barge is loaded with steel sheet piling to be used in a flood control project at Channahon. (Lewis University Canal and Regional History Special Collection.)

Sheet piling is being unloaded from a barge along the Illinois Waterway. (Lewis University Canal and Regional History Special Collection.)

These images show the CCC dock on the Illinois River at McKinley Woods. (Lewis University Canal and Regional History Special Collection.)

A view of the parking area with a trench dug for drainage tile. (Both pictures, Lewis University Canal and Regional History Special Collection.)

Seen here is the CCC constructed turnout retaining wall along the I&M Canal near Channahon. Phil E. Frederick, project superintendent for company 630 wrote of the work in this area, "The development has been not only to promote the public use of these various parks, but, also to safe guard and increase the valuable nature resources." (Lewis University Canal and Regional History Special Collection.)

Lock 6 from below is pictured here in July of 1934. (Lewis University Canal and Regional History Special Collection.)

The rebuilding of lock 6 at Channahon: Note the Lock Tender's house and the tent erected by the CCC workers in the background. (Lewis University Canal and Regional History Special Collection.)

This view from July 1934 shows the excavation from the spillway. (Lewis University Canal and Regional History Special Collection.)

In July 1934, the enrollees constructed a spillway at Channahon. Phil E. Frederick, project superintendent for CCC company 630 at Brandon-Morris, wrote "The larger [dam], a structure 250 feet in length built of stone and steel sheet piling, diverts the clean water of the DuPage River into the lower level of the I&M Canal, the contaminated water of the upper lever having been removed a thousand feet above by means of a spillway and by-pass canal." (Lewis University Canal and Regional History Special Collection.)

This view is from above Lock 6, where the enrollees repaired the lock and added a valve. (Lewis University Canal and Regional History Special Collection.)

This entrance sign to McKinley Woods was representative of the many that the CCC constructed. (Lewis University Canal and Regional History Special Collection.)

At McKinley Woods, the enrollees placed log posts and rail barriers to safeguard natural resources by restricting motor vehicles to certain areas. (Lewis University Canal and Regional History Special Collection.)

Enrollees cleared brush adjacent to the bridge over Aux Sable Creek. (Lewis University Canal and Regional History Special Collection.)

This photograph documents the location for a spillway near Channahon. (Lewis University Canal and Regional History Special Collection.)

The two photographs on this page document the progress on the spillway near Channahon. (Lewis University Canal and Regional History Special Collection.)

Planting trees was a major occupation for the CCC. The group was unofficially known as "Roosevelt's Tree Army." (Lewis University Canal and Regional History Special Collection.)

In Illinois alone, the CCC was responsible for planting 60 million trees for erosion control and reforestation. (Lewis University Canal and Regional History Special Collection.)

Edward J. Hjorth, Superintendent of Company 612, Willow Springs, noted that "For a number of items pictures were taken only after work was done, but it is obvious that the condition of these various sites were totally different because of the fact that the area occupied by this project was untouched for many years before the current Emergency Conservation Work program was put into effect." (Lewis University Canal and Regional History Special Collection.)

This image documents Route 6 near La Salle and the Texaco gas station. (Lewis University Canal and Regional History Special Collection.)

Fred Hendershot, Project Superintendent for Company 613, wrote about the picnic and trail side structures, saying "The purpose of these is to furnish resting places along the trails which afford a view of particular interest or beauty." (Both pictures. Lewis University Canal and Regional History Special Collection.)

The "Lonesome Trailers" from Camp 631 in Romeoville performed on the radio. (Courtesy of National Archive.)

Seven

CCC
LOCAL LEGACY

On the local level, the Civilian Conservation Corps had a significant impact on the communities along the I & M Canal. The benefits were manifold. Much has been made of the money that the enrollees sent home, usually around $25 month. For the family at home, not only was there additional money, but also one less mouth to feed.

The enrollees spent some of their discretionary income in the communities. The companies were also encouraged to buy supplies locally, such as lumber or food items. Finally, the park projects improved the appearance of local areas and provided recreation for the residents. Many amenities would remain long after the camps were gone. All of these brought benefits of the CCC presence to the local community. With so many camps in the area, the communities along the I & M Canal were in a better position to survive the reversals brought on by the Great Depression.

The CCC companies brought some excitement to the local area. The men from the camps played baseball, hosted dances, and occasionally dated local girls. The images featured here highlight the recreational amenities made by the CCC, which included picnic shelters, trails, and swimming areas. Many of the pictures featured here were taken in 1940. They show local residents of Romeoville (Romeo) at a swimming area constructed in 1934 out of a stone quarry. Located between Lemont and Lockport, the swimming area eventually fell into disrepair and the property was bought by an oil company in the early 1980s.

Projects like those pictured here can be found across this nation. They improved the quality of life for millions of Americans. For many who grew up after World War II, the rustic appearance of these facilities came to be what was expected of a National or State park experience.

All images are courtesy of Mabel Hrpcha.

These "CCC boys" returned to camp after "A Hard Days Work."

These were some of the young men whose work left local residents a wonderful place to swim and picnic. They built areas that became a vital part of public recreation and a large amount of Depression era labor was devoted to this kind of development.

Local residents called this The Shelter House. It was built along the route of the canal. Mabel Hrpcha said "It was a great place to sit and rest and talk."

The footbridge provided expanded access to the local area. This kind of work displayed a growing historic pride. Rose Marietta stood on the footbridge, while Mary Fracaro bravely stepped out onto the stone piers. The footbridge was near the shelter and spanned the I & M Canal.

The CCC built a "Kiddie Pool" on the east side of the local stone quarry, which was named after the Santa Fe Railroad nearby. As the camp reported in July, 1933, "Some of the people in the surrounding towns have been contacted partly by myself and partly by my foremen and we have to our satisfaction had very commendable remarks about the improvements done. The relations between these natives and the men in camps are good."

The public swimming area brought people together. It reflected an effort during the Great Depression to combat the turmoil of the time. Rose, Alice and Helen Pounovich posed on the stone terrace adjacent to the swimming area.

The use of locally quarried limestone reflected the area's history. Skilled supervisors trained the young men to create works of considerable merit. In this case, it provided seating for Mabel Fracaro and Mary Pesavento.

Rose and Helen Pounovich stood in back of their sisters Martha and Mary, who lounged on the bench.

Local historian Mabel Hrpcha took advantage of many of the sites constructed by the CCC near her home. Her photographs from 1940 captured the local enthusiasm for the swimming area.

The weighty picnic table provided the setting for Lorraine Monroe's sunbathing. Unlike some CCC projects, such as monumental amphitheaters, this swimming area was well used.

Eight

CCC

ALONG THE I&M TODAY

This book surveys the accomplishments of the Civilian Conservation Corps in Starved Rock State Park and along the I & M Canal. Although not comprehensive, it provides a sense of the scope of these efforts which transformed the landscape. The structures stand as testimonials to the young men and to the communities that embraced them. Through the large scale efforts of the CCC, the route of the canal and parks adjacent to it were given a unified purpose as a recreational corridor. The structures that remain harken back to the pioneer period, as both used local timber and limestone for construction. Visitors to this area continue to explore and discover both the remains of the old Illinois and Michigan Canal and those of the Civilian Conservation Corps.

Many CCC enrollees went on to the Armed Services during World War II. The war halted many of the elaborate plans for the canal. In the 1960s and 1970s local interest in the canal increased. Then in 1974, the old canal route was renewed as the Illinois & Michigan Canal State Trail was created. Each year this unique resource has welcomed thousands of visitors to its parks and interpretive programs at Channahon, Gebhard Woods, and Buffalo Rock. In 1984, the area received recognition with the creation of the Illinois & Michigan Canal National Heritage Corridor, the first National Heritage Area designated by Congress.

Photographer John Voss has captured reminders of the work of the CCC. For more than a decade Voss has viewed the Illinois and Michigan Canal National Heritage Corridor through the lens of his camera. Every thematic study that Voss has presented demonstrates his artistry in capturing his subject in just the right light. From the small seating areas to the mammoth fireplace at Starved Rock Lodge, the photographer's sensibility has guided him to just the right vantage point. His work provides a glimpse into the range of structures that remain along the canal and are available for visitors today. Both private and governmental agencies have restored many of the stone structures and installed information signs and commemorative plaques. Recently a group installed a statue, popularly know as Iron Mike, to commemorate the work of the CCC.

Images are courtesy of John Voss.

This view shows a footbridge over the I & M Canal. It connects to the west side of the canal. The CCC filled in part of the canal bed through Lockport, narrowing its 120 foot width.

Enrollees built this shelter in Lockport on the site of the Hydraulic Basin.

This shelter with its long, flat roof is adjacent to the I & M Canal in McKinley Woods. The CCC performed most of the early work to create this park. Visitors who hike and bike along the canal can access the park. This park is operated by the Forest Preserve District of Will County.

Frederick's Grove Shelter at McKinley Woods features a pump in the foreground and a limestone fireplace.

This CCC shelter was built along Aux Sable Creek, which is located midway between Channahon and Morris. It is typical of the many smaller trail shelters.

The is the Nettle Creek Aqueduct in Gebhard Woods State Park.

School groups hosted by the Illinois Department of Natural Resources often use the Highpoint Shelter at Gebhard Woods. It is also popular on weekends.

Enrollees built this fireplace and shelter in Gebhard Woods.

Standing atop the legendary rock, Voss photographed Starved Rock Lodge and Conference Center.

John Voss took this winter view of Starved Rock Lodge. The tree trunk sculpture is a reminder of the Native Americans who lived in the area for generations.

Three plaques at the entrance to the lodge commemorate the work of the CCC in the park.

An interior view of the lodge is seen here.

The famous fireplace in Starved Rock Lodge was constructed by the CCC.

This statue, popularly known as Iron Mike, commemorates the dedication and spirit of the young men who served in the Civilian Conservation Corps from April 1933 to July 1942. Dedicated June 3, 2001, the statue, at Archer Avenue and Willow Springs Road, stands as a testament to the CCC and their families.